THE WHITE ROSE DIES

Miles Tudor

A Tudor Sovereign Publication

THE WHITE ROSE DIES.
A Tudor Sovereign Book.

PRINTING HISTORY.
First published by the Tudor Sovereign Publishing Company 1991.
357 Hook Rise South, Surbiton, Surrey KT6 7LW.
First Edition April 1991.
Second Edition July 1991.
Revised Edition May 1993.
Reprinted December 1994.

The portraits of Richard III and Henry VII are reproduced in this book by kind permission of the National Portrait Gallery.

Cover Design: Copyright © Terence Hack.

Cover photo: Alter Ego, 13 Borough Road, Kingston-on-Thames, Surrey KT2 6BD.

Printed and bound by Anchor Press Ltd., 62 Red Lion Road, Surbiton, Surrey KT6 7QQ.

To my wife Ann,
my son Simon and my daughter Joanne
for all their patience and forbearance
while I was rolling my eyes to heaven
in creative anguish
and
to dear Molly who never saw the finished work.

ABOUT THE AUTHOR.

Born 1934 in Surrey, he was educated at the local Grammar school before joining HM. Customs & Excise.

He then saw service with R.A.F. Fighter Command, after which he joined the Metropolitan Police, retiring in 1980 with the rank of Chief Inspector.

Following on his passion for history, he formed a company specialising in personally conducted historic tours for overseas visitors. In 1990, a small publishing offshoot was added to the company, concentrating largely on historic publications.

He lives with his wife in Surrey. His sports now are squash, golf and swimming; his interests are playing guitar, reading and music of all kinds.

Miles Tudor is a pseudonym drawn from an old family name.

CONTENTS.

INTRODUCTION.

PART ONE: *THE FACTS, AND THE MYTHS OF TIME.*

PART TWO: *THE INVESTIGATION.*

INTRODUCTION.

Any book about the House of York's demise inevitably becomes the story of its last three members - the Princes in the Tower and their uncle, Richard III.

Without doubt, the disappearance and murder of the Princes remains to this day, the most baffling and fascinating murder mystery of all time, with their uncle, Richard III being generally held over the centuries to be the obvious perpetrator.

And yet, in almost every century since then, there have always been small voices expressing doubts about his guilt. In this book I have gathered the facts, the discrepancies, the myths and the questions that arise from them. They are presented as accurately and impartially as is possible so that a considered judgement can be made.

The task facing all honest researchers before writing anything about Richard III is that one must straight away put the record right respecting the quite inaccurate and scurrilous defamation of his character by the Tudor historians - and a century later by Shakespeare; in so doing one could easily be accused of bias, but it is nevertheless so important that the risk has to be taken.

A balanced and historically accurate assessment of Richard is included later in the book which shows him in a far from unfavourable light; but that said, his innocence is by no means proved and in the end, he must still be lined up with the others as a suspect.

There are a number of facts and incidents throughout the book which might seem totally unconnected, but this is not the case, and they need to be retained in the mind for the final summary. Some are historical facts, others are behaviour patterns or actions which are totally out of character with the personality of the person involved or the particular situation, and would surely activate the antennae of any modern-day police officer investigating the matter. Where these occur, I have shown them in bold italics for greater emphasis, for they will certainly need to be recalled when we come to sum up. I have similarly emboldened all dates in order that the chronological unfolding of the events may be easier followed.

The elder prince, though never crowned, was in fact, constitutionally and legally accepted as Edward V for the 10 weeks before he and his younger brother Richard disappeared for ever, but in order to avoid confusion with their father Edward IV and their uncle Richard III, I have largely referred to them throughout as "The Princes" or "the boys".

In writing this book, I have drawn on my experiences in conducting many historic tours over the years. Much of the book's content is based directly on the questions I am most frequently asked, and so I hope to have been able to anticipate and include the answers to most, if not all, the questions that this murder mystery might conjure up in the reader's mind.

And if the reader, in journeying through this medieval "Whodunnit", experiences even a fraction of the fascination and excitement which I did in researching it, my time will have been well spent. May I wish you Bon Voyage.

May 1993   Miles Tudor.

PART I
THE FACTS AND
THE MYTHS OF TIME.

CHAPTER 1.
DISTANT THUNDER...

On **9th. April 1483**, the 40 years-old Edward IV of England, quietly, and with little warning, passed away.

To all eyes England, prior to his death, had seemingly entered a period of thankful stability having just come through the 30-year trauma of the Wars of the Roses (the cousins' war) between the House of Lancaster whose emblem was the Red Rose and Edward's House of York represented by the White Rose.

The House of York had finally emerged victorious and Edward of York was back on the throne again as Edward IV. Henry VI, the weak, and periodically insane, Lancastrian king had been put to death as had his son and (more importantly) their recent ally the mighty Earl of Warwick.

Edward had been a striking man and a natural leader; standing over six feet tall, fair-haired, vital, confident, an excellent commander and a shrewd statesman, he was well able to keep his barons in order. He left two sons (the 12 years-old Edward and the 10 years-old Richard) and five daughters to ensure the succession - quite enough it was thought even in those days of high mortality. The future had still looked calm and assured.

On the other side of the coin however, Edward IV could be impetuous, greedy and given to laziness; he was also an effective womaniser, a quality which for some reason often raises men in the eyes of their peers but one which was to rebound so tragically on his sons' subsequent claim to the throne and their eventual murder.

Edward IV's younger brother, Richard of Gloucester (later Richard III), and William, Lord Hastings had stayed loyally with

Edward throughout all their tribulations and flight to the continent. On their return to England, Richard had been sent to rule the north of England and Scotland on Edward's behalf - a task he fulfilled with competence, firm but fair justice, and wisdom.

Between Edward and Richard some years earlier, had been the middle brother, the weak George, Duke of Clarence who was as disloyal and dangerous to both of them as he could be. There is no doubt that he was intensely jealous of their close relationship which had been forged when they had been forced to flee the country from the Lancastrians some years earlier: George, the Yorkist, had chosen to change sides and stay.

He had been the loose cannon - inadequate, totally unpredictable, envious, harbouring grudges, and in his search for power and recognition, forever attempting politically dangerous liaisons with, or attempts to marry into, European powers hostile to his brother Edward.

Eventually, in *1478* George had embarked on a series of actions that could no longer be ignored: he had firstly tried to effect a marriage with Mary, the only daughter and sole heir of the powerful Charles the Bold of Burgundy knowing full well that Edward was in the delicate process of negotiating an alliance with Charles the Bold's sworn enemy, Maximilian of Austria.

He had then blatantly defied the jurisdiction of Edward's Courts, setting up his own, and in addition - although never officially charged with it - he had been suspected of being party to the rumours that Edward IV was illegitimate and that therefore he (George) as the next brother down should be king. This unsubstantiated allegation, if true, would have had momentous constitutional implications, and would certainly have disqualified Edward IV and his children totally from any claim to the throne.

A geneticist, or indeed even a lay observer, would have seen considerable merit in the allegation, if he had turned his eyes from the exceptionally tall (6 feet 3½ inches) and fair Edward towards his brother Richard, 10 years younger, below average height, lean as a whip, dark and brooding - but such a comparison could be a two-edged sword, because the disparity could equally have suggested that it was Richard who was illegitimate.

If either Edward or Richard were illegitimate, then George's height and colouring would be of considerable interest in determining which of the two might be the odd one out. The few useful portraits left of George and contemporary writings would suggest that his colouring and hair were fair - like Edward's; but on the other hand, an examination of what is accepted as his bones in the Clarence vault at Tewkesbury Abbey suggest his height to have been about 5 feet 5 inches - much nearer Richard's height. Not much help there then.

In the end, this particular rumour appears to have been dismissed as just another of George's malicious and unfounded mischiefs.

However, he had far over-stepped the mark this time and he had been arrested, found guilty of treason in respect of the other matters, and sentenced to death. Edward had been reluctant to carry out the sentence when the anger had passed, and had to be pressed by Parliament. Eventually on *17th. or 18th. February 1478*, George was executed in the Tower, rumoured "...drowned in a butt of Malmsey wine...".

In addition to being sentenced to death, not only were all George's lands and titles taken from him and from his heirs too, but they also lost their rights of succession to the throne. This brought Richard several steps nearer the crown as George's children would have ranked above him.

But in time, this major event passed into history and by *1483* the only misgivings many observers felt were the positions of great power Edward had granted his wife Elizabeth's ruthlessly ambitious family (the Woodvilles).

Quite apart from arranging many advantageous marriages for them and thereby ensuring their acquisition of lands, wealth, and position, he had more dangerously allowed them to gain control of almost every political and military power base there was.

At the time of his death the Woodvilles had gained controlling influence of the court and the council (that important inner cabinet of the king's advisers); they also controlled the Tower of London, the arsenal, the King's treasure, the fleet and above all, control of the new young king and his younger brother.

Still this nepotism had been of no real matter while Edward IV had been alive, except to those who had been passed over. Although Edward had become increasingly casual and permissive where the Woodvilles and their ambitions were concerned, his strength and the laws of treason ensured that they were of no danger to the throne; and with Edward's two healthy young sons rapidly approaching their teens and their legal coming of age, there seemed no real problem.

Nevertheless, looking ahead, Edward had effectively excluded all the Woodvilles from the one position that legally, carried absolute power over all; that was the position of Regent, or Lord Protector of the king and realm. This post is always created when a king has an heir who is a minor; should the king die the Protector "advises" the young monarch who technically and ostensibly is still making all decisions in the normal way. In practice, the Regent's power is absolute and he can overrule even the young monarch; however as soon as that monarch becomes of age, the legal powers of the Regent terminate abruptly and totally.

Perhaps being more aware of the Woodvilles' shortcomings than we give him credit for, Edward had turned his eyes to the north and appointed his trusted younger brother the 30 years-old Richard of Gloucester SOLE protector and guardian of the princes and unwittingly - in quite different ways - placed all 3 in considerable (and eventually fatal) jeopardy.

CHAPTER 2.
A COUNTDOWN TO ANNIHILATION.

Most of the events in Part I of this book are pure fact, disputed by no one - layman or historian alike, whether Yorkist or Lancastrian.

And yet when we examine and interpret these facts again in greater detail - as we shall in Part II of the book - some surprising aspects start to emerge which put a quite different slant on matters.

Within 10 weeks of his father's death, the older Prince (12 years-old Edward) had been removed from the throne without being crowned, a situation soon to be followed by the highly suspicious disappearance of both him and his younger brother from the Tower *in circumstances which would suggest strongly that they had been murdered.* Two weeks later saw the accession of their uncle, Richard III of Gloucester to the throne.

When Edward IV died, it certainly caught all parties unawares and the principal characters were far flung. His son, the 12 years-old Prince Edward, was at Ludlow Castle near the Welsh border with his maternal uncle Earl Rivers and his half-brother Lord Richard Grey - both Woodvilles. Richard of Gloucester was in the north of England.

The Woodvilles immediately sought control through the prince and, quite unlawfully, began issuing orders in council - not in Richard's name but in their own.

The situation was quickly assessed by the intensely loyal Lord Hastings, the late Edward IV's Chamberlain and Chief of Guard. His loyalty had transferred undiminished from Edward IV to the son, Prince Edward; in addition, he clearly saw through the Woodvilles, whom he mistrusted. He therefore, sent urgent word to Richard.

Meanwhile Richard on his part, had seen the dangers only too well. Unlike the Woodvilles, he was almost a stranger to the prince having spent a greater part of his life ruling the north of England for Edward; the Woodvilles on the other hand were "family" and well known to the prince who, for that reason alone

5

could reasonably be expected to side with them against Richard in any future clash.

Richard must have been a very worried man. Even if he could have kept control for the time being, that would have ceased completely when the young king reached 15 and automatically assumed absolute power under statute to make his own decisions. When that time came he would in all probability choose to be advised by the Woodvilles to Richard's considerable (and possibly fatal) detriment, for in those days, opposition was often dealt with by a trumped-up charge of treason and execution.

Meanwhile, on *29th. April 1483,* both parties (the Woodvilles escorting prince Edward, and Richard's) were making their way south to London and converged at Stony Stratford in Northamptonshire. Here, as a first step to curtailing the Woodvilles' power, Richard took charge of the young king, arrested the two Woodvilles - Rivers and Grey, who were later executed - and continued on to London with the prince.

Shortly after, Elizabeth Woodville the princes' mother (and the deceased Edward IV's queen), hearing of the imprisonment of her brother and son at Stony Stratford fled into sanctuary at Westminster with the younger prince (10 years-old Richard of York), and with her daughters and Thomas Grey, Marquis of Dorset - her son by her previous marriage.

On *4th. May 1483,* Richard escorted the prince into London with full and due respect, and went ahead with arrangements for the coronation to be held on *22nd. June 1483.*

The young Edward had by then become King Edward V by proclamation and acceptance, although he had not at that time, been crowned, nor indeed did he ever have a coronation.

Regarding the coronation, it should be noted that the constitutional appointment of a monarch is quite complete at that moment of proclamation to, and acceptance by, the people; colourful though it is, a coronation is merely the ceremonial acknowledgement of the appointment.

Meanwhile the young Edward was taken to the Tower of London to await his coronation, *but there is no record that he ever again left it.* It is important to note though, that at that time the Tower was not a prison but the principal royal residence in the City and indeed, in the country. On *10th. May 1483*, the Council officially and unanimously confirmed Richard as Regent and Protector.

On *5th. June 1483,* Richard issued final, detailed instructions for the young Edward's coronation on *22nd. June* - just 17 days ahead.

Then on *8th. June* there occurred a startling turn of events; *Robert Stillington - Bishop of Bath & Wells and the late Edward IV's Lord Chancellor - gave evidence in Council that he had been witness to a pre-marriage contract between Edward IV and a Lady Eleanor Butler before the marriage to Elizabeth Woodville in 1464.* If true, this would automatically invalidate the Woodville marriage and consequently render the princes illegitimate. As the succession cannot normally travel through an illegitimate line, Richard would be the only legal claimant.

As this was the sole event on which Richard's claim to the throne was to hinge, the laws pertaining then for dealing with such a situation need some examination. In those days there were two forms of marriage, and one of them, the pre-contract existed alongside the ordinary marriage - the latter being little different from the present day ceremony. A pre-contract however, was simply a promise to marry, either verbal or written, but when it was followed by the couple going to bed together, the pre-contract became as binding in canon law as any marriage.

Had the pre-contract actually existed it was of itself quite sufficient to debar the second marriage and the princes' right to succession, but it seemed altogether too opportune an accusation to many people. In addition, it would have come as no surprise to anybody if Edward IV had acted as alleged, therefore one has to ask if this allegation was indeed false but chosen because it would have been quite in character and so easily believed.

Although most people accept that this was probably a trumped up allegation to gain power, there is a doubting minority who do not. They cast their minds back to the execution of the middle brother, George (see page 3) in *1478* and feel that his actions cited in the charges then were no worse than many others he had perpetrated in the past - and he hadn't been executed for those.

They couple this with the fact that in *March 1478*, immediately after George's execution, *this same Stillington was imprisoned in the Tower "...for some words uttered prejudicial to the king and his state"* and remained there until the *20th. June* following, when he "cleared" himself before Council after paying a ransom for his release. Unfortunately, nowhere in the official records does it show what Stillington's "words" actually were.

However, this minority asserts that these two matters are too near to be mere coincidence and that Stillington's imprisonment at that time had to be because he had revealed the secret marriage with Eleanor Butler to the insufferable George. Had he done so, of course, then it would have been a veritable fuse to a powder keg, for George would not have rested until he had he had attained the throne and would therefore have had to be silenced.

All this would suggest most strongly that the pre-contract had existed, but it is also a very dangerous course of going back in time with a theory and hanging it onto convenient facts - a very dubious and unsafe practice and with not a shred of evidence.

Return to historical fact shows that *Stillington had been the ONLY witness to the alleged pre-contract and that Lady Eleanor Butler had died - too conveniently perhaps - in a nunnery in Norwich in 1468.* Weak evidence it might have been, but on those few dubious facts alone Parliament accepted the illegitimacy of Edward's children and eventually passed an Act - Titulus Regius - bastardising the princes, making Richard king and changing the course of English history.

CHAPTER 3.
THE STRUGGLE FOR POWER AND FRIENDS FALL OUT.

Whatever the truth or otherwise of Stillington's allegation, the end result could only benefit what must have been a much relieved Richard. He was now firmly in the driving seat without having to worry about the future goodwill of the now deposed Edward V and his younger brother; in the same stroke he had also totally neutralised the influence of the Woodvilles, whose future power moves now that Richard was king, could now only be regarded as treason - punishable by death.

On *9th. June 1483*, Stillington repeated his allegation to the Lords in Parliament from which a report was prepared to place before Parliament itself when it re-assembled on *25th. June 1483*.

On *13th. June 1483*, a further development took place when Richard made a surprise visit to the Tower of London and there arrested Lord William Hastings, Cardinal John Morton and Lord Thomas Stanley for conspiracy against him. Lord Hastings was executed almost immediately, but most unwisely the other two were later released.

The powerful Lord Hastings had been honest, intensely loyal to the young prince, and no lover of the Woodvilles: his break with Richard was further evidence that Richard was about to usurp the throne - a course which Hastings simply could not condone.

His execution shook London to the foundations and certainly stopped any other critics dead in their tracks - as it was no doubt meant to; only weeks previously Hastings had been working closely with Richard against the Woodvilles and yet his death came from this quite unexpected quarter "...killed not by those enemies he had always feared but by a friend he had never doubted" (Mancini - see BIBLIOGRAPHY).

Sparing Stanley and Morton however, was an act which Richard was later to regret deeply. At least Hastings acted through loyalty, but the other two were supporters of the ever-threatening Lancastrian survivor, Henry Tudor, Earl of Richmond (later Henry VII) and both were very dangerous men to leave alive.

Morton, a lawyer and churchman who had been the late Edward IV's Bishop of Ely and one of his political negotiators in Europe, had always been Richard's bitterest enemy. If Richard remained on the throne, he (Morton) was finished. He was therefore conspiring for Henry Tudor, exiled in France, long before he landed in England and ruled as Henry VII. Morton was later appointed Henry's Archbishop of Canterbury and became a leading administrator.

Lord Thomas Stanley - together with his brother Sir William Stanley - both ostensibly on Richard's side, were in due course to lose Richard the battle and his life at Bosworth Field; Lord Thomas by not joining in at all, and the more impetuous Sir William by changing sides and attacking Richard on the flank at the crucial moment in the battle.

Add to that, the fact that Lord Thomas Stanley was Henry Tudor's step-father and still married to Henry's mother Margaret Beaufort - an ever-active conspirator in her son's quest for the throne - and one marvels that he had not been seized and executed before.

However, on *16th. June 1483*, Cardinal Bourchier, the then Archbishop of Canterbury, persuaded Elizabeth Woodville to release her son Richard (the younger of the two princes) from sanctuary to join the young Edward V - his older brother - in the Tower; *he too, is thought never to have left it again.*

On *22nd. June 1483*, the day the young Edward should have been crowned, a Dr. Shaw, brother to the Lord Mayor of London, preached an open-air sermon at St. Paul's Cross re-iterating Bishop Stillington's allegations; the following day, the Duke of Buckingham, making a similar speech to a group of eminent London citizens, emerged to play his first public role in the affair.

On *25th. June 1483*, Parliament re-assembled and considered the implications of Stillington's evidence; the allegation of bastardy against the young king and his brother was upheld and Richard was asked to become king: he accepted and was formally acknowledged by the Council.

Throughout June and most of July, the young princes were seen less and less in the Tower grounds, after which they were never seen again - certainly strong circumstantial probability that the boys had met their end at this time.

On *6th. July 1483*, Richard was duly crowned and left London on a royal progress; as far as can be ascertained Buckingham, Richard's second-in-command since April, was left in London. *It should be noted that Buckingham's high office as Constable of England gave him jurisdiction over the Tower of London and over the Lieutenant of the Tower, Sir Robert Brackenbury; it also gave him power to enter freely.*

On *29th. July 1483*, Richard arrived in Gloucester and was joined by Buckingham. *At about this time, a most serious rift occurred between Richard and Buckingham: there is no official reason recorded.* Some historians postulate that this was the time that Richard had killed the princes without consulting Buckingham, and that this had brought about the quarrel; others venture the theory that it could just as easily (and probably more likely) have been the other way round. *Whatever the reason, Richard never spoke to, nor saw, Buckingham again.*

There were a number of contemporaneous rumours at the time that Richard had killed the princes (the historians Dominic Mancini and Philippe de Commynes, and the French Chancellor in a speech at Tours, in France in 1484); likewise that Buckingham had killed the boys (Commynes again in his "Memoires", in the "Chronicles" of Jean Molinet and in the "Historical Notes of a London Citizen 1483-88") *None of them were more than rumours and no specific time, date or place of the murders was quoted as there was in the much respected Sir Thomas More's account.*

Sir Thomas More does more than just postulate. In his "History of Richard III" completed some 30 years after the event, he not only emphatically pinpoints the princes' disappearance as the time of the their murder, but also gives a most categoric and graphic account of how Richard sent a letter to his friend Sir Robert Brackenbury, Constable of the Tower, to kill the princes and that when he refused, Richard sent Sir James Tyrell to take over the Tower for the night with orders to kill the princes, and this he did. *Sir Thomas even describes with absolute accuracy the exact place where the bodies were eventually found some 200 years later.* (His possession of this last piece of information is very significant, as we shall see later).

Having said all that, there was still yet another unsubstantiated rumour that both boys had been transferred to Middleham Castle, Richard's stronghold in Yorkshire, and not killed at all.

However, shortly after their altercation, Buckingham left Richard and went on to his estates at Brecon in Wales (where Morton was imprisoned on Richard's orders). In October Buckingham changed sides, and a rebellion led by him in support of Henry Tudor gathered pace in Wales but was quickly put down: Buckingham was captured and executed.

At the same time as Buckingham's rebellion, Henry Tudor and a small fleet had sailed from Brittany with the intention of meeting up with him. He arrived off Plymouth, but instead of the rebel force he expected, he found a contingent of Richard's men waiting for him and quickly sailed off again without landing.

Meanwhile as the traumatic 1483 came to an end, the last act was played out in France. On Christmas day in Rennes Cathedral, the exiled Henry made an oath to take the Crown of England and to marry the princes' older sister Elizabeth.

CHAPTER 4.
WAITING FOR HENRY AND THE WHITE ROSE DIES FOR EVER.

1484 was barely under way when on *23rd. January,* parliament formally passed the Statute of Titulus Regius, the act which officially laid out the Princes' illegitimacy and acknowledged Richard's claim to the crown.

In the light of Henry's sworn undertaking at Rennes, there was little doubt of his intentions and for the remainder of Richard's short reign, most of his time was spent in preparing for Henry's inevitable invasion.

By the end of *March 1484*, Elizabeth Woodville had emerged from sanctuary with her daughters, all of whom were warmly received at Richard's court. *She and her family voluntarily attended Richard's social and court functions. She also wrote to her only surviving son by her first marriage - Thomas Grey, Marquis of Dorset - urging him to return from exile in France "...and make his peace with Richard". Even more remarkable is her apparent absence of anger towards, or accusation against, Richard - the man who had ostensibly killed her two sons only a few months earlier.*

Then, on *9th. April 1484* - a year to the day since Edward IV died - came the death of Richard's only legitimate child and heir, the 10 years-old Edward Prince of Wales. This latest death marked the almost total collapse of the House of York in the space of a year, and now left Richard its last, lone legitimate survivor.

To remedy this he knighted his bastard son John and also his nephew Edward, the son of his disgraced late-brother George, Duke of Clarence; in addition, he also restored lands and title to Edward and appointed him heir to the throne.

From this time until his death Richard spent the greater part of his time at Nottingham, a central position from which he could reach any of the coasts should Henry invade. A number of attempts to have Henry extradited from France were a failure

Meanwhile Richard continued his enlightened legislation which had made him so respected when he had ruled the north for his brother; among the acts was one abolishing 'benevolences', the extortionate practice whereby 'gifts' were obliged to be made to the king without the sanction of Parliament.

Nevertheless he was still losing considerable popularity and support; one of the principal reasons was that the division between the north and south of England was a very real one on every front - almost as though they were two countries; each mistrusted the other totally and the nobles in the south could see their positions being surrendered to Richard's friends from the north, and they were most unlikely to take that lying down. An indication of Richard's situation too, was that there had never been a king from the north, and Richard, due to the time he had lived there, was very much a northerner.

One of his last acts in *1484* was to prepare a proclamation against Henry Tudor and all his adherents.

1485 proved an ominous year for Richard: to add to his personal burden his wife died, aged 28, on *16th. March 1485*, and Henry's invasion was believed so imminent that on *22nd. June 1485*, Commissions of Array were issued to every county for armed men to be ready at an hours notice and the proclamation against Henry was renewed.

On *7th. August 1485*, Henry made his long-awaited landing at Milford Haven in South Wales where he had a large measure of support from the Welsh chieftains and by forced marches, his army - eventually numbering some 5,000 - reached Shrewsbury within the week. *All throughout the march the princes' probable deaths had not, somewhat surprisingly, been used as a rallying cry.*

By the *20th. August 1485*, Henry had arrived at Atherstone, 5 miles from Sutton Cheney near Market Bosworth where the final battle was to be fought.

Richard's army of about 10,000 was not quite ready and in addition he was relying on having its numbers augmented by two groups of 2,000 and 3,000 men under the command of Lord Thomas Stanley and his younger brother Sir William Stanley, respectively. These last troops commanded by the Stanley brothers were crucial for they would undoubtedly swing the outcome of the battle in favour of whomever's side they chose to join.

Lord Thomas Stanley had been one of the conspirators with Lord Hastings and Cardinal Morton at the Tower two years previously, and whom Richard had unwisely released (see pages 9 and 10). Although both the brothers were looked on as staunch supporters of Richard, the fact that Lord Stanley was married to Margaret Beaufort, mother of Henry Tudor, must have made him a dubious risk to say the least.

Add to this that when Richard had previously ordered Lord Stanley and his troops to join him, Stanley had prevaricated that he was ill from the "sweating sickness" and unable to come immediately.

At the same time, Lord Stanley's son, Lord Strange, tried to escape from Richard's court and when questioned, admitted that he and his uncle Sir William Stanley had been in communication with Henry; the boy was held hostage by Richard to ensure his father's continuing co-operation.

What must have further unnerved Richard was the knowledge that at Atherton - on the eve of the battle - Henry had had a private interview with the Stanleys to win them over to his side, but had on the face of it, been unsuccessful.

It was to this background of uncertainties and dangerously dubious loyalties that Richard went into battle on *22nd. August 1485*. The Stanley brothers, even after the battle lines were drawn up, were to be found a little distance away to one side - either holding back to see which side would win, or perhaps waiting there by arrangement with Henry.

The battle had barely started when Richard on high ground, saw Henry riding towards the Stanleys who were still a little distance away; perhaps fearing they would be persuaded to join Henry, Richard made a sudden and seemingly reckless charge down the hill at the head of his troops towards Henry in a gamble which came only yards short of success.

Whatever Richard's shortcomings, cowardice was not one of them; despite his slight stature the momentum of his charge was such that he cut his way in so close to Henry that he had already killed William Brandon, Henry's standard-bearer and thrown to the ground the immensely strong Sir John Cheney riding alongside Henry.

Henry was able to hold Richard off just long enough for Sir William Stanley to attack from the flank. Richard was unhorsed, surrounded and killed and the battle was over; Henry was just 29 years old and Richard, 32.

Richard's body was stripped, spoiled and tied naked to the back of a horse and conveyed ignominiously to Leicester where after 2 days public display, it was buried at the church of the Grey Friars nearby. His tomb was later desecrated and his remains scattered.

The death of Richard, the last Plantagenet king, was also the death of the white rose and the House of York.

But to say that the House of York and all its aspirations had died, is not to say that all its principal members were necessarily dead; we must not easily dismiss the two young princes in the Tower.

The strong probability, of course, was that they were dead at this time; Richard had every reason to kill them, for while they lived they would always be a potential threat to him.

But one thing which emerges when one reads about Richard is that - either through humanity, weakness or sheer stupidity - he had a long history of not killing those he should have removed. In fact, if we discount the princes themselves, he only killed four people on his journey to the throne, a remarkably small number in those days.

So as we go into the next chapter which charts the start of the mighty Tudor reign, we should just hold on to the whisper of a rumour that the princes might not be dead but only imprisoned, for some rather strange events occurred in the reign of the new king, Henry VII.

CHAPTER 5.
THE ACCESSION OF HENRY AND AN ODD TURN OF EVENTS.

It must be realised that Henry's claim to the throne was very weak to say the least, and in view of this, he immediately busied himself with what all usurpers needed to strengthen their claim - the issue of a Bill of Attainder against the previous king.

A Bill of Attainder is a constitutional device and a proper, formal Act - often propagandist - passed by Parliament, in which is laid out all the crimes and evils of the previous king. It had a two-fold purpose: firstly to convince the people that his removal had been necessary, but equally important to justify any trial and execution of his surviving supporters or those who might rally round him (or his heirs) in the future.

Undoubtedly, Henry's outstanding trump card against Richard was the disappearance of the princes: if murdered, a crime so loathsome that it would form the principal and, by far, the most effective accusation in the Bill of Attainder. If the bodies of the princes could also have been produced (and somebody surely, must have known - and be only too pleased to point out - where they were buried) then the case against Richard would have been unequivocally complete.

However, no bodies were produced and in the Bill of Attainder, the only reference (contained with the other broad accusations, and given no particular emphasis) which could possibly pertain to the princes' murders, was the general phrase "...the shedding of infants blood"

The princes were not mentioned by name, either as being dead, or even simply missing, and, stranger still, there is no record of any enquiry or search for them.

After his coronation in October, Henry set about successfully uniting his own House of Lancaster with the remnants of the crushed House of York so that all chance of another civil war between them in the future would be obviated.

This he accomplished on **18th. January 1486** when, in keeping with his undertaking made in Rennes Cathedral some two years previously, he married Elizabeth of York - daughter of Edward IV, niece of the deposed Richard III and older sister to the two missing princes.

At the same time he had repealed Titulus Regius, that Act of Parliament which in 1483 had formally declared the princes illegitimate and appointed Richard king; he also forbade that copies of it should be read or kept.

Now Henry, in normal circumstances, would have welcomed such an Act, for the princes were even more a bar to his claim than they had been for Richard's. However, the problem was that the same Act had also debarred their sister Elizabeth (as it did all of Edward IV's children) and he badly needed her legitimacy to strengthen his own weak claim; the Act therefore had to go.

The country settled down under Henry, Elizabeth became pregnant, and as far as the fate of the princes was concerned, they were still missing, presumed dead, and fast fading from people's minds.

And then in the summer of 1486 occurred the first of a very strange series of events - all purely circumstantial, all apparently unconnected, individually all explainable, too vague to form any reliable conclusions from, and yet taken all together, thought-provoking to say the least.

The first event concerns one Sir James Tyrell, the man whom historians accept - together with his servants Miles Forest and John Dighton - physically carried out the murder of the princes *but on a date unknown.*

Tyrell was certainly no common criminal and already held a number of very high offices under Henry, as indeed he had under Richard III.

On 16th. June 1486 he received a general pardon, although the reason is not recorded; such pardons only absolved actions taken BEFORE they were granted.

Then on 16th. July, just 4 weeks later, he received yet another general pardon; such pardons are not uncommon, but two so close together were unheard of.

The obvious, and probably correct, inference drawn by a number of historians, is a strong likelihood that he had committed some heinous crime or undertaking very soon after the first pardon to necessitate a second so soon after. Some (notably Sir Clements Markham in the 19th. Century) have openly said that this was when the princes were murdered but it has to be said, there is not the slightest scintilla of actual evidence that this was so.

On 30th. September 1486 at Winchester, Elizabeth - attended by her (and the princes') mother Elizabeth Woodville - gave birth to Henry's heir, Prince Arthur.

The second event occurred when the two Elizabeths, mother and daughter, returned to London with the new royal baby in the late winter of 1486 or early in 1487. Almost at once a most serious and unexplained clash occurred between Elizabeth Woodville and Henry.

It has been conjectured that if the princes had been up to that time only imprisoned, but then killed on Henry's orders while she was at Winchester, she would not have learnt of it until she returned to London, and that here at last was the eruption of anger and emotion one would expect from a mother towards her sons' murderer - which had been so remarkably absent towards Richard.

However, we must not lose sight of the fact that it could also have been simply a family quarrel; I am sure that bitter dissension between a man and his mother-in-law was as common then as now.

Nevertheless, almost immediately after, at a great council held by Henry at Sheen Palace near Richmond in February 1487, he stripped her of all her lands and titles and confined her in the Abbey at Bermondsey until her death there 5 years later.

The official reason given was that she broke her promise to him when he was exiled, by coming out of sanctuary at Westminster Abbey and delivering her daughters - including Elizabeth, now his queen - into Richard's hands (see page 13).

This was quite patently absurd for these very same allegations against her could equally have been made in March the previous year when Henry had freely given her the very same lands and titles - so that clearly wasn't the true reason. There was a rumour that she had also been involved in the Lambert Simnel conspiracy against Henry; but that's all it was - a rumour, and was not mentioned in the official record of the proceedings.

The third event concerns Tyrell again; on 23rd February 1487, he was ordered by Henry to surrender all his Welsh lands and titles and was recompensed by equivalent lands in Guisnes, France; he never again lived in England until his execution in London in 1502 some 15 years later.

It has been advanced that his being sent abroad was connected directly with his killing of the princes some months earlier at the time of his double pardon, and was to get him out of the way; but again, such a theory is entirely unsupported by any evidence.

In *1502* Tyrell was induced to come to England by Henry on the promise of a safe passage, but on arrival, was promptly arrested for conspiring with the Yorkist Edmund de la Pole, Earl of Suffolk against the king.

It was while he was being interrogated that he is said to have verbally confessed to killing the princes in the Tower. No statement was taken *nor was the date of the murders ever revealed. Tyrell - the one man who could solve the mystery of whether Richard or Henry had ordered the murders - was not put on trial for this offence* and was beheaded at Tower Hill on *6th. May 1502* for the original treason only.

The final scene in the saga of the princes was enacted a little under two centuries on; *in 1674 workmen discovered 2 sets of bones in a chest buried under a staircase of the White Tower in the Tower of London - exactly in the place Sir Thomas More had described.* They were assumed (correctly as it turned out) to have been of the two princes and removed to Westminster Abbey for proper burial.

In *1933*, the bodies were exhumed and examined by a Mr. Tanner, Keeper of the Muniments at the Abbey and Professor Wright then President of the Anatomical Society of Great Britain who was only able to say that the skeletons were simply of two children (the sex could not be determined), the eldest being between 12 to 13 years of age, and the youngest between 9 and 11 years - which would have tallied with the princes age when they disappeared.

More conclusive evidence however, came to light when in *1983/4* Dr. Jean Ross, then a senior lecturer in Anatomy at the Charing Cross Hospital Medical School was able to isolate rare, but similar, anomalies in the number of teeth and also in the structure of the skull in each of the skeletons.

This proved decisively that the two skeletons were at least related. In addition, the same anomalies had also been found in another known 15th. Century skeleton in the princes' family - the strongest evidence yet that these remains were of the two princes; that other skeleton was of the 8 years old Lady Anne Mowbray, a distant relative, and wife, of the younger prince.

RICARDVS · III · ANG · REX ·

Richard III, 1452–1485

Henry VII, *1457— 1509*

PART II.
THE INVESTIGATION.

CHAPTER 6.
THE SUSPECTS.

We now have in our possession all the facts, the myths and the propaganda that history can provide; it is only by how accurately we interpret them and perhaps by our detective abilities that we can arrive somewhere near the truth.

It is accepted fact that the actual murders were carried out by one Sir James Tyrell with others, but the true culprit would be the king in power at the time - or someone acting with his authority and knowledge.

The main suspect had always been Richard III but latterly as more documents were unearthed Henry VII - the succeeding king - was brought further into the frame. However there is also a third whom many historians either gloss over or fail to mention at all - namely Richard's right hand man, the Duke of Buckingham.

This omission may be based on the age-old (and normally acceptable) practice of simply regarding the actual assassin as a tool of the monarch; however, we shall see that Buckingham was anything but a tool, and had more than sufficient power and autonomy to act in his own right.

It would be useful at this point to consider the respective characters of all three so that we may better judge the probability of their guilt - or otherwise.

RICHARD III.

The last Yorkist king and the last Plantagenet. For many years he ruled the north of England ably and justly for his brother Edward IV to whom he had always shown unswerving loyalty and affection.

Known posthumously as Richard Crookback or Crouchback: firmly believed by many people to have been evil, calculating and sadistic; to have had both a withered arm and a hunch back; to have gone about dispensing evil and hurt for the sheer joy of it and to have brutally murdered his brother's children - the Princes in the Tower.

Such a savage caricature flies in the face of recorded historical fact. Whilst he must always remain one of the main suspects for the murder of the princes, the record shows him to have been courageous, fair-minded, loyal, a patron of scholars, pious and apparently with no previous ambition to the throne: he certainly did not have a hunch back nor was either arm withered - deformities written about him by Sir Thomas More alone (and later Shakespeare) both under Lancastrian regimes.

He was nevertheless capable of swift and ruthless action when required although his tally of killing only four persons (other than the Princes) to reach the throne was modest indeed for those times.

His fatal weakness was a reluctance to act against obvious enemies whom most other kings would have executed - and he paid dearly for it: the principal examples were Bishop Morton, Elizabeth Woodville, Margaret Beaufort (Henry Tudor's mother) - all of whom were plotting against him - and most importantly Lord Thomas Stanley who, with his brother Sir William Stanley, was to go over to Henry at the crucial moment at Bosworth losing Richard both the battle and his life.

It is interesting to note that all of Richard's alleged crimes were committed between April and September 1483 - the few short months he was allied with the Duke of Buckingham: before and after that period his behaviour was without criticism from any quarter.

At the end of his reign Richard had left all the alternative heirs to the throne alive and free, as indeed were all the rest of the Woodvilles.

Certainly on his previous record, Richard would probably have been as likely to have imprisoned the princes as killed them, although in those first few weeks following his brother Edward's death, he must have been a frightened man, and if pressured enough, frightened men can easily act out of character and do terrible things. Moreover, it would have been the expected course for a usurper to kill the previous king.

The origins of the hunchback myth.

The chasm between the myth and the man is so great that it begs explanation; Richard's public relations problem was that at that time, every historian but one (Mancini) was Lancastrian writing under a repressive Lancastrian regime which did not take kindly to unpalatable fact.

But the fact remains that Richard had neither a hunchback nor a withered arm. Only two contemporaneous paintings of Richard show these physical malformations; one is held in the Royal collection at Windsor and the other by the Society of Antiquaries - both works, under infra-red examination, clearly show that the line of the shoulder and the arm have been exaggerated by over-painting at a later date.

Shakespeare's part can be easily dismissed; he was simply an Elizabethan (Tudor) playwright seeking a melodramatic plot and who probably had few real thoughts of Richard, who had died over a hundred years earlier

He got his inspiration from, and no doubt accepted as gospel, the version of Richard's character from Sir Thomas More's uncompleted "History of Richard III" published in 1513 - nearly 30 years after these events.

A word on Sir Thomas More.

Now Sir Thomas More was an entirely different matter; he was a pious family man, a massive academic revered by all, but beheaded by Henry VIII because on a point of principle he would not accept him as head of the newly formed English church above the Pope. A devout Christian he habitually wore a hair shirt in penance next to his skin but above all he was honest.

Therefore although he was the only writer who referred to Richard's alleged deformities, More would not have mentioned them unless he thought them to be true.

It is only when the dates are checked, it is revealed that *when Richard was crowned, More was only 5 years old and of necessity would have had to obtain all his information second-hand.* Therefore the source of his information needs to be sought, and - even more important - very carefully evaluated.

Research shows that at the age of 13 years he was placed in the household of the ubiquitous John Morton, Henry's Archbishop of Canterbury at that time, and a hated enemy of Richard's.

As Morton, when Richard was alive, was continually spreading malicious rumours against him, there was no reason to believe he would change when Richard was dead; so here was the almost certain origin of More's version.

If Morton had simply passed on the facts to More by word of mouth, the origin could only have remained pure conjecture, but a study of More's "History of Richard III" (laying out Richard's murderous acts) is interesting and strongly suggests that the major part, if not all, of it could even have been written by Morton himself, and re-issued by More under his own name.

Firstly it should be remembered that More was a classical scholar in both Greek and Latin, yet much of the original Latin manuscript of the book is in a Latin seemingly much inferior to More's normal authentic Latin prose.

In addition, the whole tenor of the manuscript is strongly pro-Lancastrian and is written in a style which would indicate that the writer had actually witnessed some of the events described - which clearly More could not have done.

Indeed, for what it is worth, Sir John Harrington in his "Metamorphosis of Ajax" (1596) ventures that Morton was the author, and later, Sir George Buck in his "History of Richard III" (1646) says plainly that Morton wrote "..a book in Latin against King Richard, which afterwards came into the hands of Mr. More, sometime his servant...".

*Therefore it follows that if More **had** plagiarised his uncannily accurate location of the Princes' skeletons from Morton - **Henry's right-hand man and total confidante**, it will (as we shall see), throw a whole new light on Henry's guilt in, and knowledge of, the killings.*

If an inordinate amount of time appears to have been spent on Richard, it is not to absolve him from suspicion. But for those who know him only from the More/Shakespeare version, a sense of fair play alone decrees that the record should be put right. For those more familiar with Morton's feelings of hatred towards Richard, it is equally important that one does not go too far the other way, and dismiss his very serious allegation against Richard purely as malice, for it could well be true.

DUKE OF BUCKINGHAM.

More accurately, Henry Stafford, 2nd. Duke of Buckingham. A shadowy figure; powerful, ambitious, plausible, ruthless, unpredictable and Richard's strongest ally, being virtually his second-in-command. At the time of the princes' disappearance he held the rank of Lord High Constable of England, a rank which significantly, gave him power to enter the Tower of London as he chose: more importantly he had a not inconsiderable claim to the throne, being descended from Edward III's seventh son.

Although subordinate to the claims of the young princes and Richard (descended from Edward III's fourth son) it was stronger than Henry Tudor's - the third suspect. Buckingham's claim would therefore benefit greatly from the Princes' deaths although Richard would still need to be removed later.

And that is how many observers see Buckingham's charted course, picking off all the rivals one by one as he changed sides. Joining with Richard and ensuring that the princes were removed; then leaving Richard, as he did suddenly in the late summer of 1483 when the princes disappeared (possibly murdered) with the view of joining Henry against Richard; and finally if Richard had been defeated, he would then only be left with Henry a man whose

27

dubious claim to the throne could be contested constitutionally with his own higher, legitimate claim.

As we have seen, whatever his plans were, he got no further than stage two before Richard had him executed.

HENRY VII.

A truly outstanding king and a most efficient and far-seeing ruler in every way. A tall austere man who made few close relationships, left little to chance and was the first English king to have a personal bodyguard.

He was strong, calculating, avaricious, shrewdly cautious and restrained. Unlike Richard, he suffered no qualms about imprisoning or executing opponents; in fairness, his actions were probably quite devoid of malice and simply seen as something which needed to be done.

He weakened his barons by forbidding them private armies and imposing the most harsh fines for even minor transgressions: his crippling taxation and the institution of the infamous Star Chamber (a special Court for nobles too powerful for the normal courts to deal with) ensured their complete subjugation.

He skilfully avoided war as being too costly, and built up strong protective alliances instead. His government was strong and wise and he encouraged shipbuilding and the formation of a strong navy: he also encouraged exploration of trade routes and development of commerce but above all his every move was successfully designed to increase his private fortune which on his death was enormous.

A meticulous and somewhat miserly perfectionist he gained a certain notoriety by personally checking and countersigning the royal household account books.

As for Henry's motive for murdering the princes, it must be realised that his claim to the throne was weak, and indeed whatever need Richard may have had to do away with the princes, it was nothing compared with Henry's; even if only one of them had been alive after the Battle of Bosworth, then Henry had not the slightest claim whatever to the succession. Only the deaths of both princes could open the way.

With some knowledge of the suspects concerned, and most of the facts mustered, it only remains to sift through them for the most likely culprit; it is a difficult task, for nearly all the evidence is circumstantial and that type of evidence has a habit of slipping so easily into conjecture, with all the attendant dangers.

CHAPTER 7
THE DENOUEMENT.

Let us assume first of all that the princes were killed in the summer of *1483* by either Richard or Buckingham, acting singly or in concert.

Richard the culprit?

Firstly we have to accept that at this time the boys did suddenly disappear virtually off the face of the earth, and at no time did Richard make the slightest effort to explain their whereabouts. If they were killed, then this would probably have been the time

Having said that, Richard would have had a much reduced need to kill them; he had effectively had them declared illegitimate by Act of Parliament (Titulus Regius - see page 8) by which same Act he had placed himself firmly and legitimately on the throne. Certainly, he was in nothing like the danger he had been before the Act was passed.

It is true they would have remained as a focal point for any future insurrection, but with Richard's previous record, he could be as much expected to have them kept prisoner somewhere in one of his northern strongholds as have them killed.

In any case, to kill the boys secretly at any time would seem to be a quite clumsy course of action; with the medieval infant mortality rate being what it was, the safest and least troublesome method, if the princes did have to be killed, would be to issue a series of worsening medical bulletins, then have them smothered and the unmarked bodies displayed to public gaze. The absence of forensic or post mortem skills would render that course of action quite safe and without complication.

Buckingham the culprit?

Buckingham on the other hand, could have had every reason to wish them dead. If he had intended to murder the boys while with

Richard, and then remove Richard after he had gone over to Henry, he had to get rid of the boys before he left Richard, for he wouldn't get as good a chance again.

The question (to which there is no answer) will always be did Richard, acting alone and hastily through fear, have the Princes murdered; did he and Buckingham agree to act together or lastly did Buckingham himself have the Princes murdered without consulting Richard thereby incurring his anger.

Friends fall out.

Whatever it was, there occurred this sudden and violent quarrel between them in the late summer of *1483* which was unexplained and total: it could simply have been, of course, that they were arguing over whether the boys should be killed or not. Buckingham left for Wales and they never met again.

Elizabeth Woodville and Richard

And in the midst of all this, we should not lose sight of Elizabeth Woodville, the boys' mother. Her attitude towards Richard is important; even taking into account that women had very little control over events and that Richard had removed her son from the throne, she appears to have got on passably well with him, even attending his social functions with her family and inviting her son Dorset - who had fled abroad from Richard - to return and make his peace (see page 13). Not, one might think, the actions of a woman whose sons Richard was supposed to have just murdered.

She obviously would have had little love for Richard but her singular lack of recorded anger does need explanation; indeed, if Richard had had the boys killed, then her behaviour was quite astonishing.

If it were Buckingham who had killed the boys against Richard's wishes, and Richard had been able to convince Elizabeth that this was so, with suitably sincere regrets, then her attitude was just, but only just, believable.

However, if the boys were merely imprisoned somewhere and still alive throughout the rest of Richard's reign, then her lack of anger and hostility is not at all unusual, for putting on a good face for Richard would ensure they stayed that way.

The value of imprisoning the princes.

Keeping the princes incommunicado at an unknown location might seem at first sight a pointless exercise, but it would have considerable tactical value for Richard in keeping Henry guessing.

We shall see time and time again how the princes complicated matters for Henry, and it was vital for him to know if they were still alive or not, before he invaded England; alive, they presented much greater difficulties for him than they did for Richard.

If both princes were dead, then it was a straight fight between him and Richard; if he lost, he would be executed, but if he won he would be king of England - even with his poor claim to the throne.

But consider Henry's impossible position if even only one of the princes were alive; if he lost, he would still be executed but if he defeated Richard he would then be faced with one or both of the princes, who although bastardised and debarred by Titulus Regius, could well be a focal point for other Yorkists and, if re-instated, (for acts of parliament are not necessarily irreversible) have an irrefutably stronger claim to the throne than him - and he, a Lancastrian, would still be executed.

The princes' murder not used as a rallying cry.

Buckingham when he fled to Wales in *1483*, would have known if the princes had been killed when they had disappeared from the Tower (no matter whether by himself or Richard), and this is very important. If they were already dead, he would have known where the bodies were, and would certainly have told his new ally Morton (whom he was holding prisoner in Wales on Richard's behalf); in due course Henry himself, and no doubt many others would, without a shadow of a doubt, have learnt the true facts from Morton when he eventually escaped and joined Henry in France early in *1484*.

This in turn would have led to Henry - desperately trying to drum up as much support as he could on the way to Bosworth - using the murder of the Princes as a rallying call and to the production of the two bodies as soon as he took over in London - but none of this happened (see pages 14 & 18). From this, everything seems to suggest that the boys were still alive, at least when Buckingham left Richard for Wales.

Indeed, there seems an equally strong probability from the circumstantial evidence so far, that the princes were alive when Henry became king, and if further support were needed for that view it is supplied by Henry's subsequent actions - or rather lack of them - on becoming king.

Production of the princes' bodies.

Consider his position: whatever his qualities, Henry was a usurper, moreover a usurper with a tenuous claim to the throne; it was vital that he justified his actions quickly in those first few precarious days, and what better propaganda than to produce the bodies of the princes (if they were dead) brutally murdered by Richard the man he had just ousted. But no such display of the bodies occurred (see page 18).

If there were bodies, it is not good enough to say that Henry didn't know their location; it is quite inconceivable that there wasn't somebody who could supply the necessary information.

And it is here too, that the importance of the More (Morton) authorship of the "History of Richard III" becomes very significant (see page 26); whichever was the original author, the burial place of the princes described in that book was precisely where their bones were actually found in *1674* (see page 22).

If Morton were the original author (as seems probable) or even if he only supplied the information verbally to More, this means that he knew exactly where the princes were buried - More certainly couldn't have known for himself. As Morton had been openly allied with Henry during the months preceding the invasion, it means that, if the boys really were dead and Morton knew where the bodies were, then Henry certainly knew too (see pages 26 / 27).

And if the boys were dead, there isn't a single reason on earth against Henry producing the bodies and giving them a proper burial, and every reason in favour of it; at one fell swoop he would remove all doubts that they were alive, and therefore a challenge to him, and he would at the same time sully Richard's name for ever.

Even if we give Henry the benefit of the doubt and accept that he really didn't know where the bodies were, the fact that the children were simply missing would still have been more than enough to lay their murder firmly at Richard's door.

Henry's Bill of Attainder against Richard

Add to this Henry's extraordinarily inadequate wording "...the shedding of infants blood" in his Bill of Attainder against Richard (see page 18) and there is indeed food for thought; the description of Henry's character in the previous chapter is a very accurate one - he was a thorough and precise man in all he did. Had Richard murdered the princes - his own nephews - Henry simply would not have let such an infamous crime be so vaguely referred to; he would, quite understandably, have spelt it out in large letters for the whole world to see.

Tyrell not brought to trial.

And most significantly of all, immediately after Bosworth, Tyrell was not brought to trial. Had the princes actually been murdered by him during Richard's reign, enough people would surely have known of his involvement for him to have stood trial.

Tyrell "escapes" trial again.

It is equally difficult to provide a reasonable answer - other than the obvious - to those who ask why he was again not put on trial in *1502* after he is said to have confessed to the murders (see page 21).

It is quite true that there was no legal need to try Tyrell for the killings; he had already been sentenced to death on another treason charge, and you can only kill a man once. Nevertheless, the assassination of a young king was hardly trivial and one would not have thought such a serious crime would be virtually ignored.

And if the princes had been murdered in Richard's reign, a trial would not only tidy up the record, but again could only show Henry in a favourable light; if however, they had been killed during Henry's reign and on his orders, it would be quite understandable that he would not want to put Tyrell - a man who had nothing to lose - on trial where he might give embarrassing and damning evidence.

The last five points, i.e., the boys' murders not being used as a rallying cry, their bodies not produced after Bosworth, no direct accusation against Richard for their murder, and lastly Tyrell not brought to trial (either in *1485* or in *1502*), are in my view, the most telling. Try as I might, and whichever way my thoughts turn, there seems one inescapable explanation and one only - that one, or both, of the princes were alive when Henry became king; if we accept that, then quite simply, the prima facie case of murder against him is complete.

So, what if the princes were alive?

On becoming king, Henry's intention had been to repeal Richard's act of Titulus Regius (see page 8), thereby restoring the line of succession to the boys' elder sister Elizabeth, and then to marry her and by so doing considerably strengthen his own fragile claim to the throne.

But if the princes were alive, then he had a problem to say the least, for they would always be a danger to him. He could not then repeal Titulus Regius while they remained alive, because he would re-legitimise both boys and hand the line of succession straight back to the elder prince; if he however, kept them bastardised by retaining Titulus Regius, that would also keep their elder sister Elizabeth bastardised too, and completely negate her strong, and much-needed claim to the lineage.

The alternative murder scene,

Henry's motives and choice of action were starkly clear; if he wanted to be king and restore the succession effectively to Elizabeth and their children, the very existence of the princes would have to be denied right from the start, and they would then have to be disposed of at an opportune moment. The unthinkable alternative would be for him to abandon all his plans entirely and return to exile.

Even for a strong king like Henry (bearing in mind also that he was married to the boys' sister) the moment would have to be opportune; if he did have the princes murdered while his wife was confined in childbirth at Winchester attended by her (and the princes') mother, it was probably the perfect opportunity, for he could not delay the deed for too long.

If that were the moment chosen, then all the apparently unconnected happenings would start to click into place; Tyrell's double pardon (page 20), and his being sent abroad for the rest of his life (page 21); Elizabeth Woodville's sudden unexplained anger at Henry when she returned from Winchester and his subsequent stripping her of all lands and titles before banishing her (pages 20 & 21); Tyrell's execution after admitting to the boys' murder, without even being charged and tried for such a major treason (page 21), and of course, Henry's Archbishop Morton (via Sir Thomas More) seeming to know precisely where the bodies were buried (page 12, 26 & 27) - not surprising perhaps, if he had been in at the kill.

Summary.

There can rarely have been more "Ifs" to the page than there have been in this last chapter, but even a discussion between the most academic would contain equally as many, because that is the sort of mystery it is; every person has to make his or her own judgement, for nothing can be proved conclusively.

Like most students of history I am most reluctant - and indeed ought not - to pass judgement, knowing full well that the facts which are suppressed by those in power at the time are always more important than those allowed to filter down through history; as it is, a great deal of the evidence that has filtered down is merely circumstantial - and the unreliability of that must never be lost sight of.

But that said, there are for my own part, too many unexplained loose ends and odd happenings; some that really are capable of ambiguous interpretation - and therefore doubtful, but others that in my opinion, point so unequivocally to the murders being committed during Henry's reign, that I find myself increasingly drawn to the view that he, through Tyrell, was the most likely culprit.

In requiem.

And at the end, whatever did transpire, there remains a truly tragic episode of history, inadvertently triggered by the princes' father Edward IV choosing Richard as Regent and Protector for the older prince, an act which sadly brought them into conflict with the avaricious Woodvilles; I say sadly, because they were neutralised or removed so early on, but had probably been in the fray just long enough to make Richard change course to ensure his own safety - a course which eventually took them all onto the rocks to their deaths.

BIBLIOGRAPHY.

***The Usurpation of Richard III** (De Occupatione Regni Anglie per Ricardum Tercium)* **by Dominic Mancini.**

> NOTE: Deals with events in England up until June 1483 when Mancini, an Italian cleric and historian (later Archbishop of Vienne), returned to France. Found fairly recently (1933) in the Bibliotheque Municipale in Lille by C. A. J. Armstrong of Hertford College, Oxford. An invaluable record as it is the only one written in Richard's time (1483) and not later under a Tudor regime. It is valued by historians generally for its honesty and objectivity.

Second Continuation of the Croyland Chronicles.

> NOTE: Written in 1486, author unknown but believed to have been Bishop John Russell, Richard's Chancellor. Its tone is anti-Richard but it is an important document because, whether written by Russell or not, its author was certainly at the hub of power and in Richard's Council.

***History of Richard III** by Sir Thomas More (See page 20).*

***Memoires** by Philippe de Commynes.*

> NOTE: Covers European history from 1464 to 1498. Commynes was a well-respected French politician, diplomat and historian.

***The Rous Rolls and Historia Regum Angliae** by John Rous.*

> NOTE: Rous a 15th. Century historian was chaplain and recorder to the Warwick family.

***History of England** by Polydore Vergil.*

> NOTE: Vergil was an Italian historian who came to this country at the beginning of the 16th. Century and was commissioned to write the above work by Henry VII.

***English Historical Documents** edit. by Prof. A. R. Myers (1969)*

Historical Notes of a London Citizen 1483-1488.

> NOTE: discovered by Prof. Richard R. F. Green in the College of Arms and published in 1981

***Richard III and his Early Historians** by Alison Hanham (1975)*

***The New Chronicles of England and France** by Robert Fabyan.*

> NOTE: Fabyan was a City of London Alderman; the work was published posthumously in 1513.

***Fragment of Document (Ref: MS2 M6).** held by the Royal College of Arms.*

***Marriage Litigation in Medieval England** by Professor Helmholtz (1975).*

***The History of King Richard III** by Sir George Buck.*

> NOTE: Edited by A. N. Kincaid (1979).

Chronicles of London

> NOTE: or by its Cottonian Library reference Vitellius A XVI. (15th. Century).

***English Constitutional Ideas in the 15th. Century** by S. B. Chrimes.*

INDEX.